Hidden Life

What's Living On Your Body?

Andrew Solway

Heinemann
LIBRARY

www.heinemann.co.uk/library
Visit our website to find out more information about **Heinemann Library** books.

To order:
☎ Phone 44 (0) 1865 888066
🖹 Send a fax to 44 (0) 1865 314091
🖥 Visit the Heinemann Bookshop at www.heinemann.co.uk/library to browse our catalogue and order online.

First published in Great Britain by Heinemann Library, Halley Court, Jordan Hill, Oxford OX2 8EJ, part of Harcourt Education.
Heinemann is a registered trademark of Harcourt Education Ltd.

Editorial: Nancy Dickmann and Kate Bellamy
Design: David Poole and Paul Myerscough
Illustrations: Geoff Ward
Picture Research: Rebecca Sodergren
Production: Séverine Ribierre

Originated by Dot Gradations
Printed and bound in China by South China Printing Company

The paper used to print this book comes from sustainable resources.

ISBN 0 431 189617 (hardback)
08 07 06 05
10 9 8 7 6 5 4 3 2

ISBN 0 431 189684 (paperback)
09 08 07 06 05
10 9 8 7 6 5 4 3 2 1

British Library Cataloguing in Publication Data
Solway, Andrew
Hidden Life: What's Living on Your Body?
616'.01

A full catalogue record for this book is available from the British Library.

Acknowledgements
The publishers would like to thank the following for permission to reproduce photographs:

Oxford Scientific Film p. **9b**; Science Photo Library pp. **12b, 22, 25b**; Science Photo Library pp. **4b, 6, 10a, 11, 13a** (Eye of Science), p. **5** (BSIP/Laurent), p. **7a** (Dr Chris Hale), p. **7b, 8** (David Scharf), p. **9a** (K H Kjeldsen), p. **10b** (Darwin Dale), p. **12a** (Andrew Syred), p. **13b** (Dr P Marazzi), p. **14** (Dr Jeremy Burgess), p. **15a** (Eddy Gray), p. **15b** (Damien Lovegrove), p. **16a** (Dr Tony Brain), p. **16b** (Science Pictures Ltd) p. **17** (Dr Kari Lounatmaa), p. **18** (Dr Linda Stannard, UCT), p. **19a** (Volker Steger), pp. **20a, 20b, 21** (Eric Grave), p. **23** (Biophoto Associates), p. **24** (Linda Steinmark, Custom Medical Stock Photo), p. **26** (Richard T Nowitz), p. **27** (CNRI); Tudor photography pp. **4a, 19b**.

Cover photograph of an itch mite, reproduced with permission of Eye of Science/Science Photo Library.

Contents

Any words appearing in the text in bold, **like this**, are explained in the Glossary.

Many of the photos in this book were taken using a microscope. In the captions you may see a number that tells you how much they have been enlarged. For example, a photo marked '(x200)' is about 200 times bigger than in real life.

Take a closer look

You probably think that you know your body really well. You have seen yourself thousands of times in mirrors and in photos. You know how your body looks, feels and smells. But move in close enough and your body becomes an unfamiliar landscape – a microscopic world full of hidden life.

Imagine taking a good look around your body using a microscope. As you increase the magnification, you will find more and more examples of hidden life.

Getting up close

Look at your skin at low magnification. It's covered in a network of lines and

From a distance your skin looks smooth, but under a microscope the tiny pores (holes) can be seen, as the photo on the right shows (x800). The pores lead to glands that produce sweat and oils.

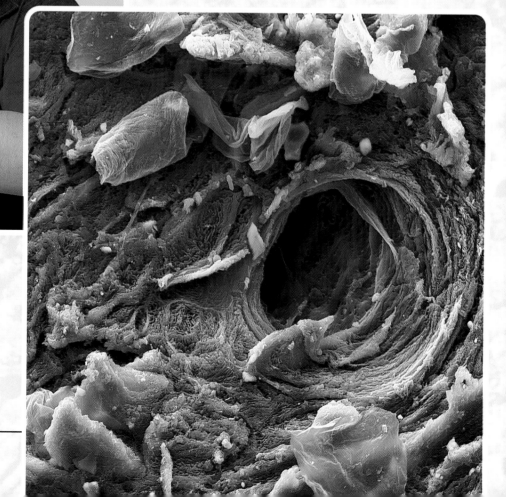

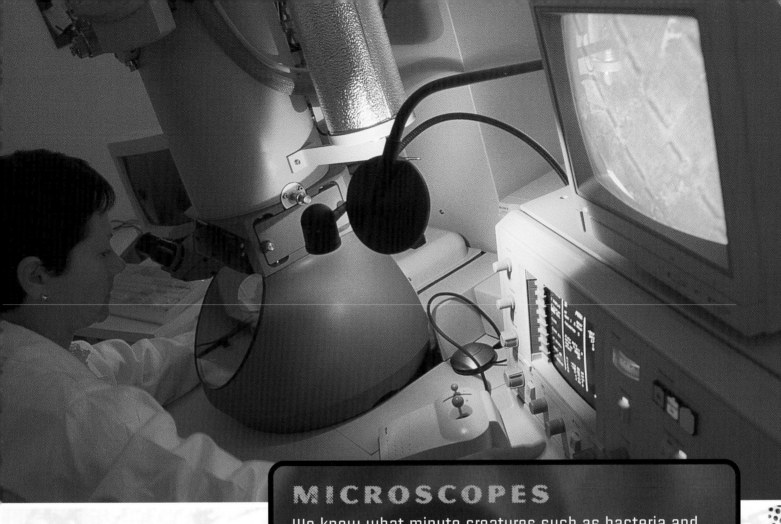

tiny holes. The hairs on your skin are like tree trunks, and the hair on your head is a forest. Tiny insects can live in this forest. Even tinier minibeasts can live on your eyelashes, eating bits of skin and oils that the skin produces.

Closer still

At high magnification, you will find that just about every part of your skin is home to microscopic creatures. Most are **bacteria** – simple living things made of just a single

cell. We think of bacteria as germs that cause disease, but most of the ones that live on your skin are harmless.

Up your nose!

Now let's increase the magnification of your microscope to 100,000 times – and poke it up your

nose! Here you will find some of the smallest living things of all – **viruses**. Outside of another living cell, viruses are just tiny packages of a few complex chemicals. But if they get inside your cells they can make thousands of copies of themselves, making you ill in the process.

Vampire insects

Have you ever had an itchy head that bothered you for days? If so, you might have had an attack of vampire insects! These terrible bloodsuckers are better known as head lice. Luckily they are very small, so they don't usually cause anything worse than itching.

Grains of lice

Lice are **parasites**, which means that they live and feed on their human **host**. Adult lice are greyish-white insects the size of a grain of rice. They have no wings, and their bodies are flattened. They have strong, hook-like claws that they use to hang on to your hair. Lice live for about a month, but they cannot survive for more than about 2 days off their host.

A human head louse (x150).

Feeding

Lice have mouthparts designed for bloodsucking. A set of curved hooks around the mouth dig into the skin when the louse is about to feed. Then two thin tubes pierce the skin. The louse's **saliva** helps the tubes go in, and prevents the blood from **clotting**.

Lice feed two or three times a day. After a meal, a louse looks reddish brown because of the blood inside it.

Louse eggs

Louse eggs are called **nits**. Females 'superglue' their eggs to hairs, which makes them hard to remove. The eggs take 8 or 9 days to hatch.

Growing up

When they hatch, young lice look similar to adults. They are known as **nymphs**. The nymphs begin to feed on blood almost as soon as they hatch. They grow quickly, and after about 9 days are mature adults.

Louse eggs (nits) in a girl's hair. The egg case has a 'lid' that pops open when the louse hatches.

A human body louse. Body lice look similar to head lice, but they only occur where people are living in cramped, dirty conditions.

GETTING RID OF LICE

Head lice don't mind clean hair, and they often get passed from person to person at school. If you do get lice, there are lots of ways to get rid of them. Lice do not like oil, so oiling your hair and combing it can get rid of them. There are also special shampoos that you can use.

jumping fleas

Head lice live in hair, but we can also get unwanted guests on our bodies. Fleas are tiny wingless insects about 2 millimetres long. They hop on to us to grab a meal of blood, and then jump off again.

Fleas on the wrong host

Fleas are **parasites** that spend some of their time in the **host**'s bedding, and only get on the host to feed. Different kinds of flea feed on different animals. The fleas that most often bite people are cat or dog fleas that jump on to a human by mistake. They take a quick meal, but human blood is not to their taste so they hop off again.

There is another kind of flea that is specific to humans. But you are unlikely to come across it unless you don't wash for a month, because they only like dirty clothes and bedding.

What do fleas look like?

A flea's body is flattened sideways, which makes it easy for fleas to move through fur. Fleas have pointed mouthparts that they use to pierce their host's skin and suck up blood.

A flea's body (x150) is covered in backward-pointing bristles. It can move forward smoothly, but if it moves backward the bristles cling to the host's fur, anchoring the flea in place.

Leaping over tall buildings

Fleas get on and off their hosts by jumping – and they have an astonishing jump. A flea can jump up to 100 times its body length. If you could do that, you would be able to jump over a 40-storey skyscraper!

Fleas don't just use muscle power to jump. When a flea bends its back legs before taking a jump, the bending motion **compresses** a thick pad of springy material at the top of the leg. When this pad is released it suddenly springs back into shape, giving the flea a tremendous boost of power.

A flea larva (yellow) coiled around fibres in a carpet. Flea larvae are blind and worm-like.

Flea lives

Female fleas lay their eggs in the nest or den of their host. In the case of dog or cat fleas, this means in your pet's bed. Young fleas (**larvae**) take a week or more to develop, then they spin a silken **cocoon**. About a week later, an adult flea emerges from the cocoon.

The most likely way for fleas to get on your body is from your pets. So if your dog or cat is scratching a lot, check for fleas!

Hitch-hiking ticks

Like fleas, ticks hitch lifts on humans and take a blood meal as they ride along. Fleas and lice are annoying, but ticks can carry disease.

Ticks are not insects, but eight-legged relatives of spiders. There are several kinds that feed on humans.

A meal a year

At each stage in their lives, ticks eat only one large blood meal, then drop off their host. Ticks go through three main stages in their lives – **larvae**, **nymphs** and adults. Each stage can take a year or more. So in three years a tick gets three meals at best. Males miss out on the last meal, so they get only two!

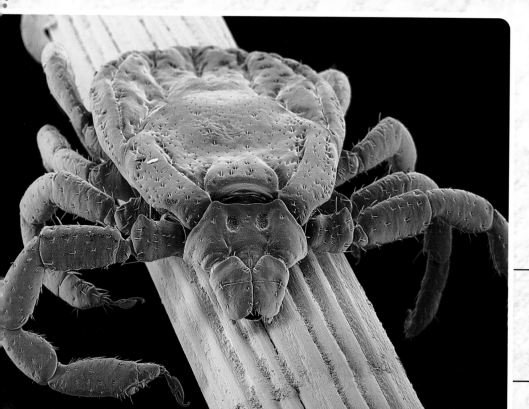

Adult deer ticks are smaller than a pinhead. This one has been magnified 25 times. Deer ticks can carry an illness called Lyme disease.

From eggs to larvae

Female ticks lay several thousand eggs. The larvae that hatch from the eggs have only six legs. To eat, a larva needs to find a **host**. So it climbs a grass stalk or other plant and waits for a host animal to brush past.

Dog ticks can pass bacteria to humans that causes a form of typhus. This dog tick has been magnified 45 times.

If a suitable animal comes by, the tick crawls on and takes a meal. Once it has eaten, the tick drops off the host, then **moults** to become a **nymph**.

From nymph to adult

Tick nymphs have eight legs. Like the larvae, nymphs look for a host, take a meal and then drop off. Some kinds of tick feed on the same kind of host animal, while others feed on a different kind of host.

After its second meal, the tick drops off and moults once again to become an adult. The adults mate, and male ticks die soon afterwards. Females take a last meal and then lay their eggs.

Ticks and disease

Usually, a tick will cause nothing worse than a sore, itchy bite. But some types of tick can carry disease. In the USA, for instance, tiny deer ticks can cause

an illness called Lyme disease. This causes a rash and flu-like symptoms, then later the joints become painful and swollen.

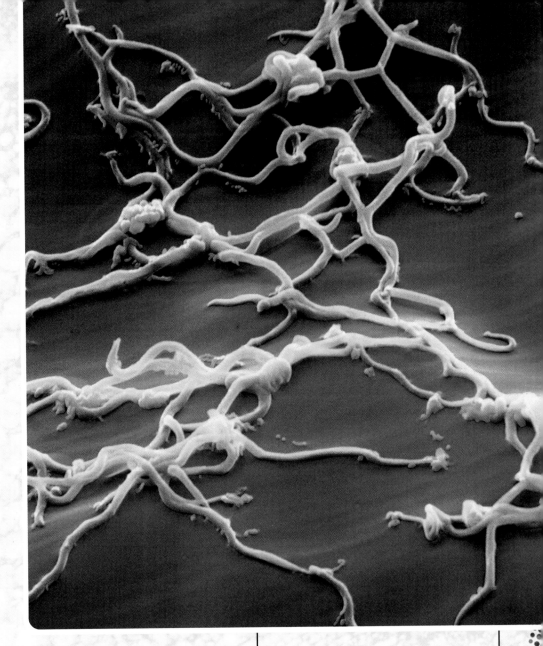

🔹 *Ticks themselves don't cause disease – they are infected with harmful microbes, which they pass on to their **host**. These stringy-looking bacteria (x9560) cause Lyme disease in humans.*

BIG APPETITES

In one meal, a tick can suck up as much as 100 times its own weight in blood. As it feeds, it pumps most of the water from the blood back into its host. If it didn't do this, it would burst!

Tiny mites

Although lice, fleas and ticks are small, you soon notice if they bite you. Eyelash mites don't bite, and they are so tiny that you may never know they are there. But their relations, the itch mites, are not so pleasant!

Like ticks, mites are relations of spiders and have eight legs. But not all mites are **parasites** or bloodsuckers.

Mites on your eyelashes

Eyelash mites, or follicle mites, are very tiny creatures that live on the face, particularly around the eyelashes and ears. They live near **hair follicles** and feed on skin and on oils produced by the follicles.

Even the cleanest people can get follicle mites – most of us have them at some time in our lives. They usually cause no harm, but doctors think that they sometimes help cause acne (bad spots) in teenagers.

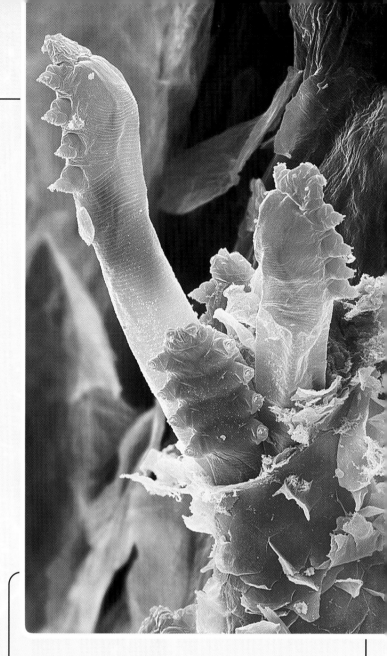

Follicle mites (x390) sticking out of a hair follicle. These mites are around a tenth of a millimetre long. The front part of the body (seen here) has four pairs of short, stubby legs.

Itch mites

Itch mites are much less pleasant than follicle mites. Luckily they are much less common too, so you are unlikely to get them unless you come into contact with an infected person.

Itch mites are about the same size as follicle mites and, like follicle mites, they eat human skin. They would be fairly harmless except that when female mites have mated, they dig tunnels into the skin to lay their eggs. These tunnels cause terrible itching. Constant scratching can cause wounds that then become infected.

Female itch mites make tunnels into the skin, especially on the hands and wrists, and lay two or three eggs each day. The tunnels can be 3cm deep and cause severe itching.

The itch mite tunnels cause wounds and scratching that then create blisters, scabs and a red rash know as scabies. Scabies can be passed on by close contact with an infected person.

Pollen up your nose

Every spring and summer, the air is filled with clouds of fine, yellow dust – **pollen**. Most pollen comes from flowers. Each flower produces clouds of pollen, some of which will reach another flower of the same kind and **fertilize** it. But the rest of the pollen gets everywhere – in your hair, on your clothes, and up your nose.

A cloud of pollen is released by Alnus cordata catkins.

Pollen grains are not living creatures, but they contain a germ of life inside them. They are the male **sex cells** of flowering plants (like the **sperm** of male animals). When a grain of pollen meets up with an egg cell from a flower of the same kind, the two join together. From this joined cell come the seeds that will be the next generation of flowers.

Amazing shapes

Pollen grains are tiny – to our eyes they look like very fine dust. But put pollen grains under the microscope, and you find that they are not simply small, round balls. The hard outer casing of each tiny grain is a marvellously sculpted shape.

Pollen grains from different plants look very different. Some have spikes all over their surface, which help them to stick to animals or insects. Flowers whose pollen is carried by insects usually have larger pollen than those that rely on the wind to carry their pollen.

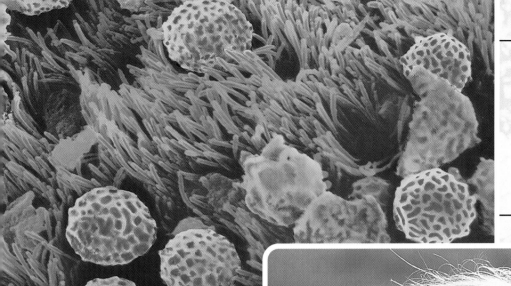

These pollen grains (x1110) are lying among the millions of tiny hairs that cover the surface of the throat. These hairs beat to and fro, and will eventually push the pollen out of the throat.

Pollen on people

At times of the year when there is a lot of pollen around, you breathe in pollen grains every time you go outside. The pollen grains get trapped in the sticky mucus that lines your nose and throat. In many people, this pollen does no harm, but some people are **allergic** to it. Their bodies act as if the pollen grains are invading germs, and the result is hay fever – a blocked nose, sneezing, and streaming red eyes. Pollen is also thought to make **asthma** worse.

Not all types of pollen cause allergies. Only small pollen grains are light enough to be carried far by the wind. Also, chemicals on the outside of the pollen affect whether it causes allergies or not.

People who suffer from hay fever start sneezing if they go outside when there is a lot of pollen around.

LONG-DISTANCE TRAVELLERS

Pollen grains from ragweed flowers are long-distance travellers. They have been found 650 kilometres out to sea and 3 kilometres up in the air.

Friendly bacteria

Did you know that your skin is crawling with **microbes**? It's not because you are dirty – washing will not get rid of them all. These microbes are not dangerous germs, but harmless residents that actually help keep us healthy.

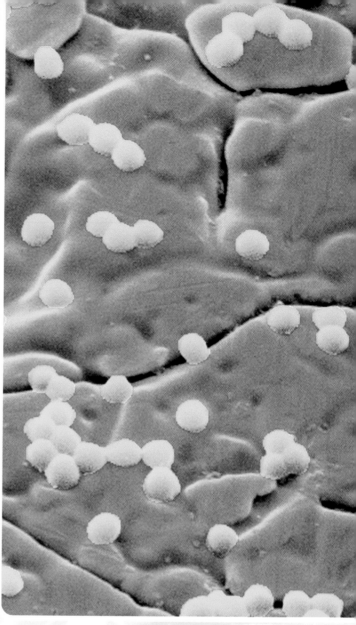

Skin infections can be caused by the bacteria Staphylococcus aureus, which often grow in clusters of small spheres (x8530).

There are about 50 different kinds of microbe living on our skin, and most of them are **bacteria**. Some bacteria are rod-shaped (bacilli), some are round or oval (cocci), and a few kinds are spiral (spirilli). The rods and spirals often have whip-like tails called flagella.

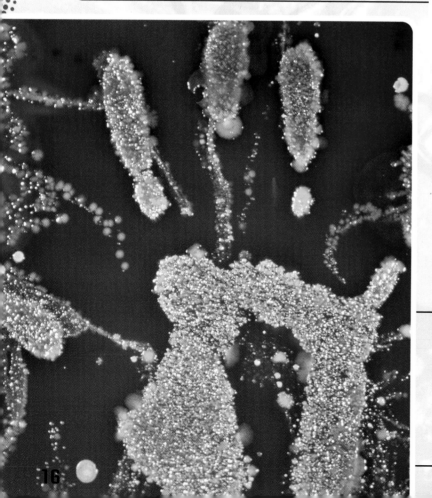

A 'bacterial handprint'. A hand was pressed on to a plate of agar gel, leaving behind some of the bacteria that were on the hand. The gel contained food for the bacteria, and after a period of time large colonies of bacteria grew all over the handprint.

Favourite places

Bacteria live all over your body – even on your eyes! But in some places there are billions, and in others only a few. To a bacterium, our bodies are enormous – as big as a whole planet. Some parts are good places for bacteria to live – warm, moist places such as armpits and between your toes. Here there may be billions of bacteria. Other parts of the body are less hospitable. The arms and legs, for instance, are microbe 'deserts', with only a few thousand bacteria per square centimetre.

Protective microbes

The bacteria best adapted to living on our skin cause us no harm. In fact they help protect us, by eating food and taking up living space that might otherwise be used by disease-causing bacteria. Scientists have found that if an animal is brought up with no microbes on its skin, as few as ten harmful bacteria can make the animal ill, whereas it would take about a million bacteria to infect a normal animal.

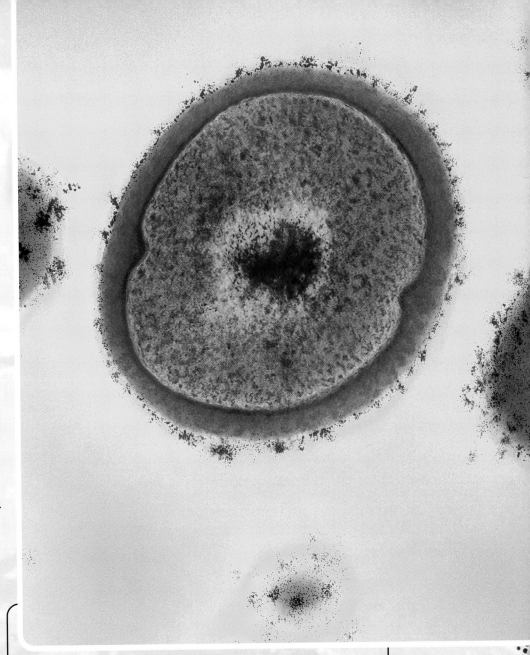

Staphylococcus aureus *bacteria, like this one (x200,980), are common on the skin.*

STINKY SWEAT

Sweaty bodies can get very smelly. For proof, just go into a changing room after a hard football match! But sweat is simply salty water produced by special sweat glands in the skin – it does not smell. The smells come from the waste products of billions of bacteria and other microbes living around your sweat glands.

Microbes in your mouth

There may be billions of **microbes** on your skin, but there are lots more in your mouth! Your mouth is a wonderful place for **bacteria** to grow. It is warm and moist, and a feast of food passes through it every day.

Over 200 kinds of microbe live on the skin, but there are almost 80 different types in the mouth. As on the skin, they take up space that could otherwise be occupied by harmful microbes.

Although the mouth is moist and there is plenty of food, the microbes don't have it all their own way. Every time you eat, you swallow millions of them, and they are killed by the strong acid in your stomach. Your saliva (spit) also contains natural **antibiotics**.

Spiral bacteria (Spirochaetes) like these are common in the mouth. Unlike other types of bacteria, Spirochaetes do not have a hard outer cell wall.

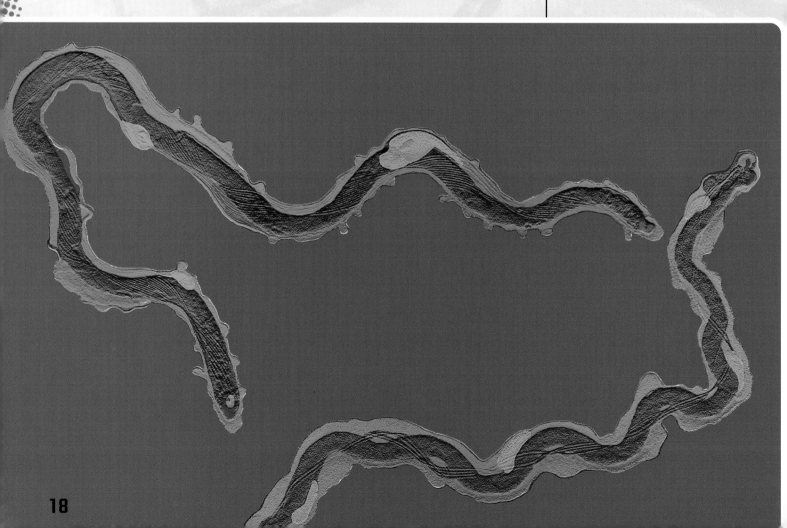

Between the teeth

The favourite places for bacteria and other microbes are the gaps between the teeth and the places where the teeth meet the gums.

A thin film, several hundred microbes thick, can build up in these places. This film is called **plaque**. Many kinds of bacteria grow here, including bacteria called *Spirochaetes*, which are not found on the skin. There are also some **yeasts**, which are a kind of **fungus**.

A tooth cut through and photographed in special light to show tooth decay.

Tooth decay

Some of the microbes in plaque do no harm. But some bacteria, in particular one called *Streptococcus mutans*, cause problems. Like other bacteria they feed on the sugars in food. But they produce acid as a waste product, and this acid can damage the hard outer covering of your teeth (**enamel**). Eventually a hole may be worn in the tooth, and bacteria can get in and cause tooth decay.

Brushing your teeth regularly stops the build-up of too many bacteria and helps prevent tooth decay.

Bacteria-hunters

Bacteria are not the only **microbes** living in the mouth. There are also some microbes that eat bacteria. These bacteria-hunters are called **amoebas**. They help keep down the number of bacteria in the mouth.

Amoebas are more complicated than bacteria. Their **cells** are like the cells that make up larger animals, not like bacterial cells. In particular, they have a **nucleus** whereas bacteria do not.

Getting about

The outside of the amoeba is a thin flexible membrane. The material filling the membrane is called cytoplasm. In amoebas this cytoplasm can change easily from being liquid to being jelly-like and almost solid. This is important for the way the amoeba moves around.

To move forward, the amoeba pushes out finger-like extensions of the cytoplasm called **pseudopods**.

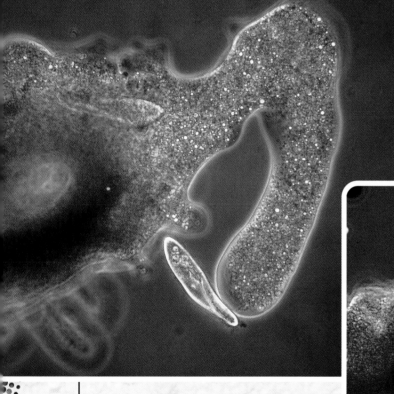

 In the photo above, an amoeba is about to engulf a microbe (bottom right of the photo). In the photo on the right, the microbe is inside the amoeba.

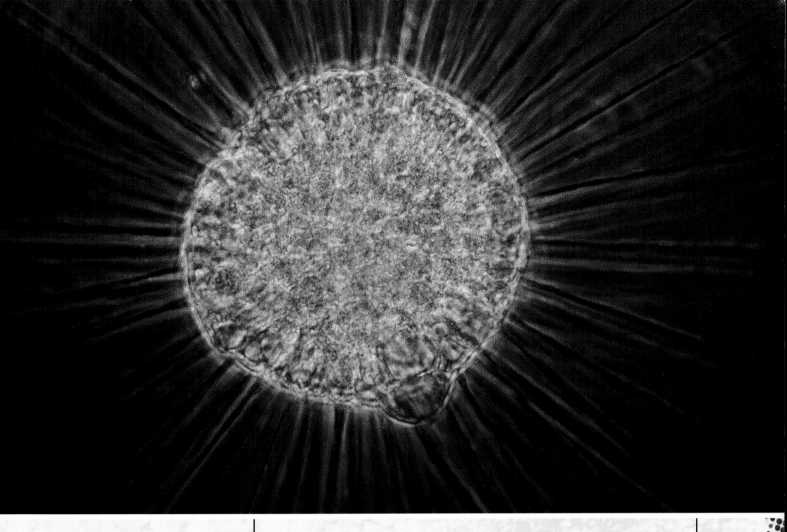

Catching bacteria

Amoebas also catch bacteria with their pseudopods. They extend long pseudopods to surround their prey without touching it. Then the pseudopods close in, until the prey is trapped in a small round 'bag' called a **vacuole**. The amoeba then digests the prey and absorbs its **nutrients**.

Types of amoeba

The amoebas that live in the mouth are part of a group called *Entamoeba*.

The kind of pseudopod an amoeba makes can help to identify it. This amoeba, Actinosphaerium eichhorni, has thin, spiky pseudopodia.

Some others in this group live in the gut, and can cause ulcers. Amoebas can also live in the ocean, in fresh water and in the soil.

Most are microscopic, but some can be up to 5 millimetres long. These giant amoebas have many nuclei, rather than just one.

AMOEBA RELATIVES

Amoebas are part of a large, loose grouping of single-celled creatures called **protozoa**. Protozoa generally need to eat food to survive, like animals, while **algae** are more plant-like single-celled organisms. There are few kinds of protozoa on the body, but some can cause diseases if they get through the skin (see page 27).

Microbe problems

Most of the time we don't notice the billions of **microbes** on our skin. But occasionally something goes wrong. **Bacteria** get through the skin's defences, and cause problems. Or microbes that don't usually live on the skin move in and take over.

Boiling up

Many bacteria live inside a **hair follicle** rather than on the skin surface. The follicle is a pit in the skin, containing the hair root and an oil-producing **gland** called the **sebaceous gland**. The oil from the sebaceous gland lubricates the hair, keeping it supple.

Normally dead cells and bacteria from the hair follicle are carried to the skin surface by this oil. But sometimes a mixture of oil and dead cells clogs up the top of the hair follicle, and it fills up with oil and cells. Bacteria also build up in the follicle, and chemicals they produce cause irritation and **swelling**. The result is a spot.

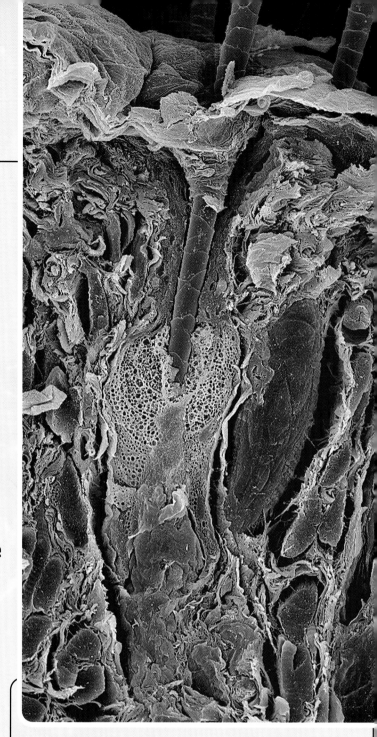

This photo of a hair follicle (x295) shows the hair (brown), the hair root (mid-green) and the sebaceous gland (the blue structure to the right of the hair root).

Everyone occasionally gets the odd spot or two. However, teenagers often get worse spots known as acne. This is because during the teens our sebaceous glands begin to produce more oil.

Fungi on your feet

Another part of the body where things can go wrong is the feet. Feet are warm and damp, which are good conditions for bacteria. The bacteria don't do anything worse than make your feet smell – although smelly feet can be pretty bad! But if your feet are hot and sweaty a lot of the time, the conditions become ideal for some kinds of **fungus**. They cause a skin disease called athlete's foot.

Athlete's foot gets its name because you normally pick up the disease in places such as swimming pools and changing rooms. It starts as dry, itchy skin between the toes. The skin then cracks, and blisters may form. If it is not treated, the disease may spread to other parts of the body.

Athlete's foot is caused by a group of fungi called dermatophytes. These fungi (shown in orange here) are made up of microscopic branching threads that cover the skin cells (in blue and yellow).

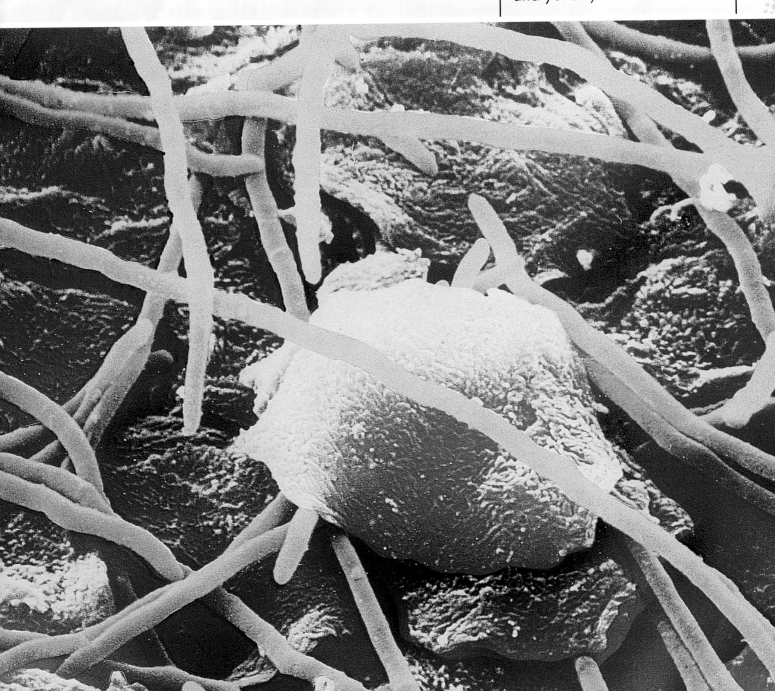

The very smallest **microbes** that live on your body are **viruses**. Viruses are incredibly tiny – they can be 100 times smaller than **bacteria**. The best place to look for these miniscule microbes is up your nose.

Many different viruses live on the inside of your nose and in your throat. As with the bacteria that live on us, most are harmless. But if we get some kinds of virus in our nose, we get a cold.

Getting a cold

We get colds by breathing cold viruses in from the air, or by touching a surface with viruses on it and then touching our noses. Colds are not caused by one type of virus – there are over 100 different cold viruses.

When you sneeze, particles are ejected from your nose at over 160 kmph (100 mph).

How a virus works

When a cold virus lands on the inside of your nose, it gets into a **cell** of the nose lining. Once inside the cell, it takes control. Instead of doing its normal job, the cell starts churning out hundreds of copies of the virus. Eventually it becomes so full that it bursts open, releasing the virus copies to infect other cells.

It takes 8–12 hours from the time a cold virus enters the nose to the release of the first wave of viral copies. This is when the first cold symptoms begin.

Self-inflicted symptoms

A cold infection usually affects only a small part of the nose, because our body's defences react quickly and many of the viruses are killed. But the

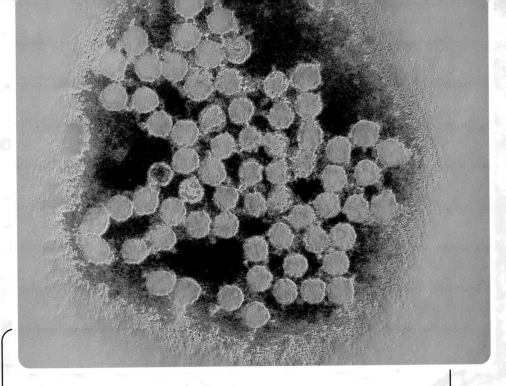

The rhinovirus is one of the causes of the common cold. Here it has been magnified 219,600 times.

body also defends itself against the virus by causing sneezing and coughing, to get the viruses out of the body. So most of the symptoms of a cold are caused by the body itself!

Chicken pox is another disease caused by viruses. As with colds and flu, the virus can be passed on when a person with chicken pox sneezes or coughs.

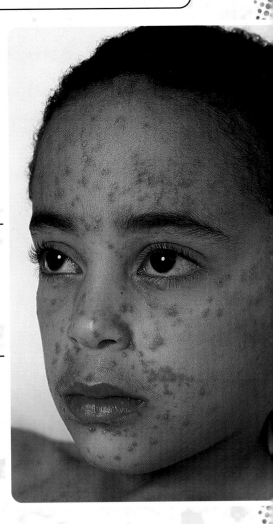

NOT ONLY COLDS

Colds are not the only illnesses caused by viruses. Flu, measles, chicken pox, smallpox, bronchitis and AIDS are just some of the many other viral diseases. As with colds and flu, the viruses for measles, chicken pox and bronchitis can be spread through the air.

Barrier-breakers

The skin is the first line of the body's defences against disease. It is hard for **microbes** to get through its many layers. But some microbes have found a way round this defence. They get themselves injected straight into the bloodstream.

A tough barrier to cross

Your skin is an excellent barrier to microbes. The top layers of the skin are made up of flattened, dead cells full of a tough substance called **keratin**.

Only female mosquitoes carry disease. Their needle-like mouthparts have no trouble piercing human skin. Males have different mouthparts and only feed on nectar.

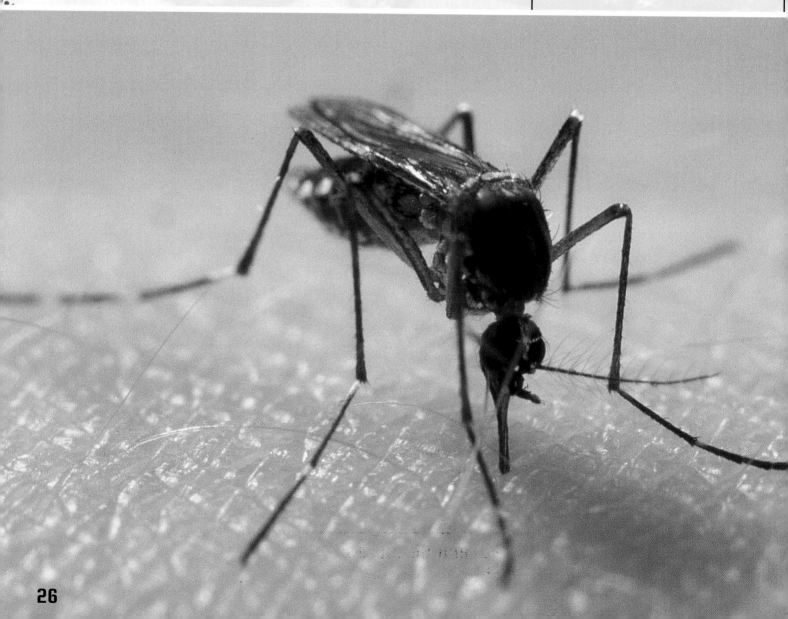

This is the same substance that your nails and the horns of many animals are made of (in nails and horns the keratin is much thicker). The cells are glued together by a kind of 'cement', and oils from the **sebaceous glands** make the skin waterproof. To a **bacterium** less than a tenth the size of a single cell, this is a tough barrier to get through.

Getting past the skin

One way that microbes get past this obstacle is through an insect bite. Some of the blood-suckers we have already mentioned, in particular ticks, can carry disease-causing microbes. They pick up these microbes by feeding on an infected animal. Ticks that cause Lyme disease, for instance, pick up the bacteria that cause this disease from infected mice. If an infected tick then bites a human, it passes the bacteria on into the person's blood.

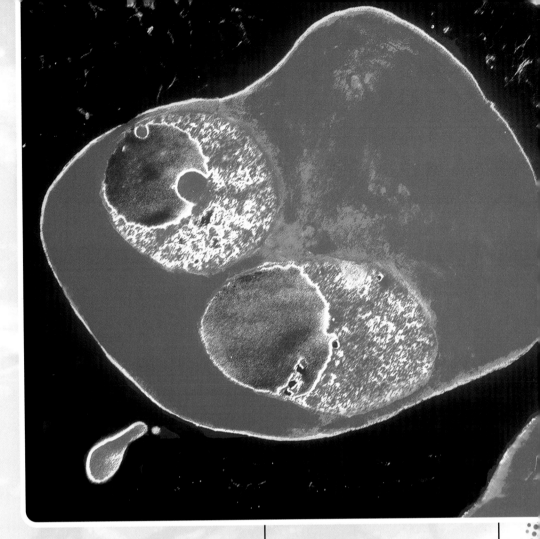

Mosquito carrier

Probably the top disease-carrying insect is the mosquito. It can carry many different diseases, in particular malaria.

Malaria is caused not by a bacterium but by a **protozoan** called *Plasmodium*. When an infected mosquito feeds on a human, it injects **saliva** into the bloodstream to stop the blood from **clotting**. The *Plasmodium* gets into the blood in this saliva.

🔴 *This red blood cell (x17,650) is from someone with malaria. It has two Plasmodium protozoans inside it. Eventually the blood cell will burst.*

In humans, *Plasmodium* acts a bit like a **virus**, getting into blood cells and reproducing inside them until the cells burst. If a mosquito feeds on a person that has malaria, it sucks up some *Plasmodium* with its blood meal. Now the whole cycle can begin again.

Table of sizes

Although all hidden life is tiny, there is a huge range of sizes. To a flea, a grain of pollen seems just as tiny as the flea seems to us!

Dog tick
5 – 6 mm

Head louse
0.7 mm

Deer tick
3 – 4 mm

Plasmodium
0.1 – 0.3 mm

Follicle mite
200 µm

These organisms are 20 times bigger than normal.

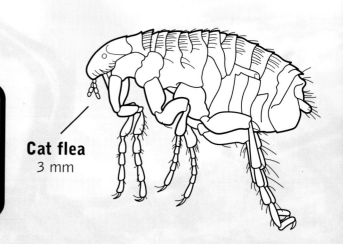

Cat flea
3 mm

HOW SMALL?

1 m (metre) = 1000 mm (millimetres)
1 mm (millimetre) = 1000 µm (micrometres)
1 µm (micrometre) = 1000 nm (nanometres)

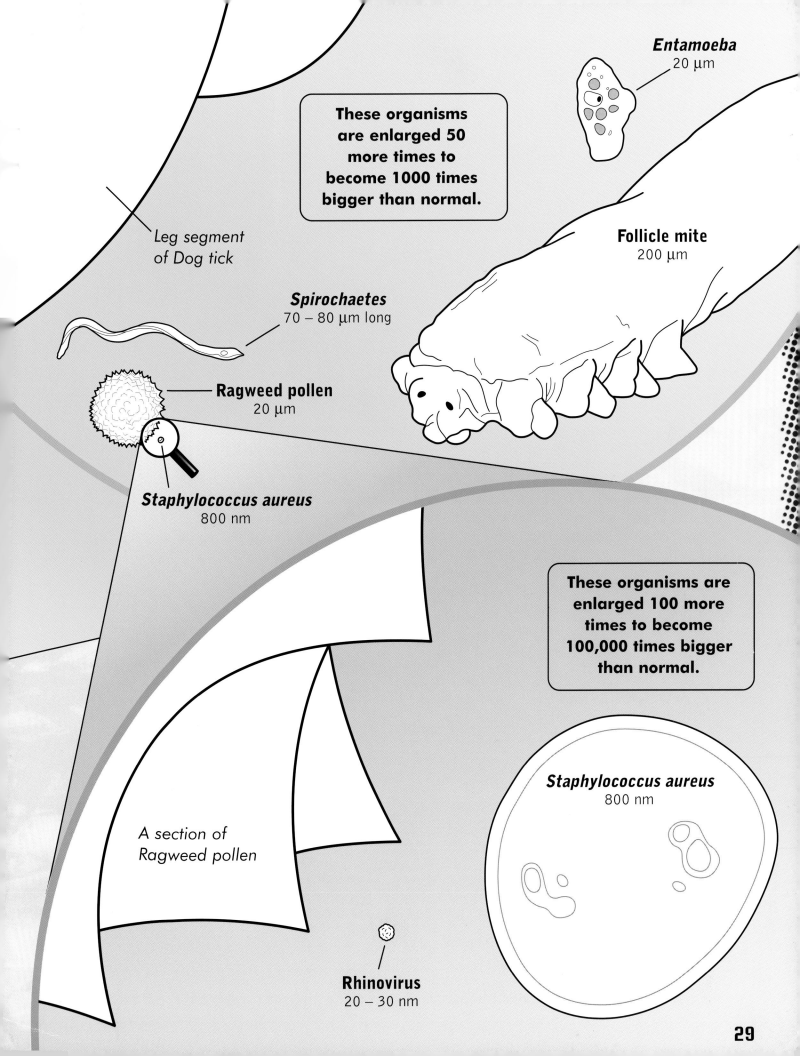

Entamoeba
20 μm

These organisms
are enlarged 50
more times to
become 1000 times
bigger than normal.

Leg segment
of Dog tick

Follicle mite
200 μm

Spirochaetes
70 – 80 μm long

Ragweed pollen
20 μm

Staphylococcus aureus
800 nm

These organisms are
enlarged 100 more
times to become
100,000 times bigger
than normal.

A section of
Ragweed pollen

Staphylococcus aureus
800 nm

Rhinovirus
20 – 30 nm

Glossary

algae large group of plant-like creatures, most of which are microscopic

allergy/allergic when the body overreacts to something that you breathe in, eat or get on your skin. It can cause sneezing, a rash or sickness.

amoeba single-celled microbes that move and catch food by sending out finger-like projections called pseudopods

antibiotic drug or natural chemical that kills bacteria or stops them from growing

asthma a disease of the lungs that causes wheezing and other breathing difficulties

bacteria very tiny creatures, each one only a single cell. They are different from other single-celled creatures because they do not have a nucleus.

cells building blocks of living things. Some living things are single cells, others are made up of billions of cells working together.

clotting formation of a solid blood clot caused by special factors in the blood. Clotting helps a wound to heal quickly.

cocoon silky, cigar-shaped case spun by many species of insect larvae to protect themselves while they change from larvae into adults

compress squash into less space

electron microscope very powerful microscope that can magnify objects up to half a million times

enamel hard outer coating of the teeth. Enamel is the hardest substance in the body.

fertilize when a special sex cell from a male creature joins with the egg cell of a female to form a new life, it fertilizes the egg

fungus plant-like living things such as mushrooms and yeasts

gland group of cells that produce a chemical or other substance

hair follicle small hole or pit in the skin which contains the root of the hair and the sebaceous gland

host animal or plant that a parasite lives on

keratin tough substance that is used to make nails, horns and hair, and is an important part of the skin

larva the young stage of some types of creatures. Larvae look different from adults, and may have to go through a changing stage in order to become adults.

microbe microscopic creature such as bacteria, protozoa and viruses

moult to shed hair, feathers or skin

nits eggs and egg cases of lice

nucleus round structure surrounded by a membrane found inside a living cell. It contains the cell's genes.

nutrient chemical that nourishes living things

nymph the young of some types of creature. Nymphs usually look similar to their parents, and change gradually into adults over several moults.

parasite creature that lives on or in another living creature and takes their food, without giving any benefit in return

plaque thin film, rich in bacteria, that forms on the teeth

pollen fine powder produced by flowers. If pollen is carried by the wind or insects to other flowers of the same kind, it fertilizes them.

protein important group of substances that are used to build structures within living things, and to control the thousands of chemical reactions that happen inside cells

protozoa single-celled creatures that have larger, more complicated cells than bacteria

pseudopod ('false foot') finger-like projection that forms when an amoeba moves

sebaceous gland oil-producing gland in the hair follicles

sex cell special cell produced by female (egg cell) and male living things in order to reproduce. If the male and female sex cells combine, a new life is formed.

sperm male sex cells of humans and many other animals

vacuole fluid-filled bag inside a cell

virus very tiny microbe that has to infect a living cell in order to grow or reproduce

yeast microscopic single-celled fungus

further reading

Awesome Bugs: Spiders and Scorpions, Anna Claybourne (Franklin Watts, 2003)

Cells and Life: The Diversity of Life, Robert Snedden (Heinemann Library, 2002)

Cells and Life: The World of the Cell, Robert Snedden (Heinemann Library, 2002)

DK Mega Bites: Microlife: The Microscopic World of Tiny Creatures, David Burnie (Dorling Kindersley, 2002)

Horrible Science: Microscopic Monsters, Nick Arnold, illustrated by Tony de Saulles (Barbour Books, 2001)

The Illustrated Wildlife Encyclopedia: Bugs & Minibeasts, John Farndon, Jen Green and Barbara Taylor (Southwater Press, 2002)

Microlife: A World of Microorganisms, Robert Snedden (Heinemann Library, 2000)

Websites

Cells Alive! (www.cellsalive.com)
Pictures, videos and interactive pages about cells and microbes. The How Big? page shows the sizes of creatures from mites to viruses.

Virtual Microscopy (www.micro.magnet.fsu.edu/primer/virtual/virtual.html)
On this interactive website you can pick from a selection of samples, adjust the focus, change the magnification, and use a whole range of powerful microscopes.

Microbe Zoo (www.commtechlab.msu.edu/sites/dlc-me/zoo/)
A site about strange creatures from the world of microbes.

Microbe World (www.microbeworld.org/home.htm)
Information, pictures, movies and activities exploring the world of microbes.

Index